MONEY ORIGAMI

by Won Park

THUNDER BAY
P·R·E·S·S

Thunder Bay Press
An imprint of the Baker & Taylor Publishing Group
10350 Barnes Canyon Road, San Diego, CA 92121
www.thunderbaybooks.com

Watch Won Park in action, folding a koi fish. Visit the Web site http://orikane.com/members/2010/03/money-origami-koi-carp-instructions-video/.

Developed by The Book Shop, Ltd.
Instructions and diagrams by Marcio Noguchi.
Box, book, and origami papers designed by Kyung-Ah Son.
Photography by Kyung-Ah Son.

All notations of errors or omissions should be addressed to Thunder Bay Press, Editorial Department, at the above address. All other correspondence (author inquiries, permissions) concerning the content of this book should be addressed to The Book Shop, Ltd. New York, New York 10010.
www.thebookshopltd.com.

ISBN-13: 978-1-60710-281-6
ISBN-10: 1-60710-281-1

Printed in Thailand.
1 2 3 4 5 15 14 13 12 11

TABLE
OF CONTENTS

ORIGAMI TERMS

Valley fold -------------

Mountain fold -·-·-·-·-·-

Crease _____

Hidden ·······················

Preliminary base

Waterbomb base

Petal fold

Swivel fold

Rabbit ear fold

Squash fold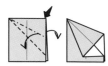

Inside reverse fold

Outside reverse fold

Closed sink

Open sink

Spread sink

Repeat steps here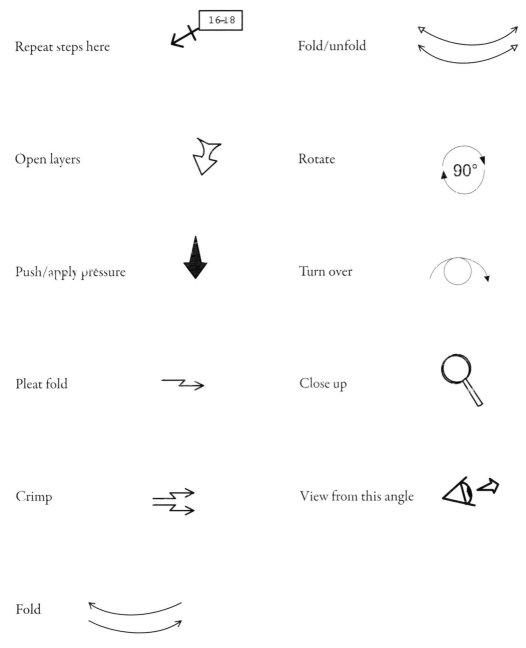

16–18

Fold/unfold

Open layers

Rotate

90°

Push/apply pressure

Turn over

Pleat fold

Close up

Crimp

View from this angle

Fold

DOUBLE CRANE

1 Fold in half. Unfold.

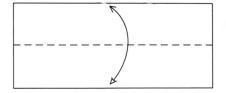

2 Fold in half. Unfold.

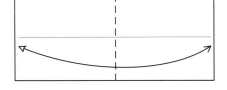

3 Fold the edges to the crease.

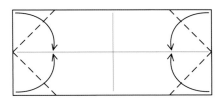

4 Fold the corner to the edge. Unfold.

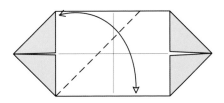

5 Fold the opposite corner to the edge. Unfold.

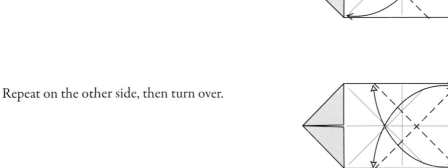

6 Repeat on the other side, then turn over.

7 Fold edge to edge. Unfold.

8 Fold through the intersections of the creases. Unfold. Turn over.

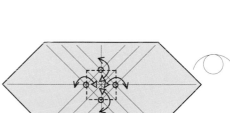

9 Crease between the reference points.

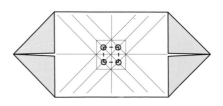

10 Mountain fold in half.

11 Inside reverse using existing creases.

12 Inside reverse using existing creases.

13 Unfold.

14 Spread squash fold using existing creases.

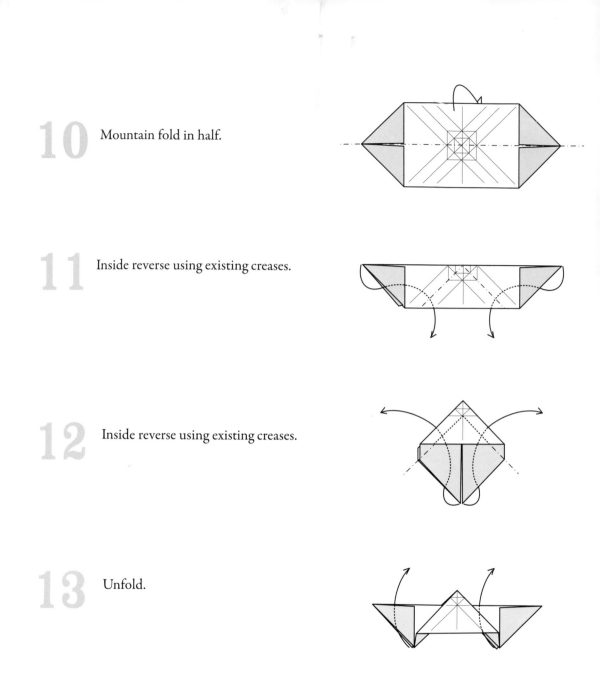

15 Fold the corners along the folded edges.

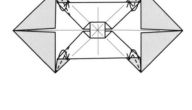

16 Pull out the paper trapped inside and swivel fold as shown. Tuck the edges behind the spread squash.

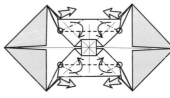

17 Turn over.

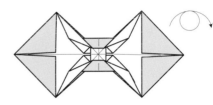

18 Fold and unfold. Turn over.

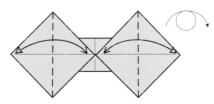

19 Fold and unfold.

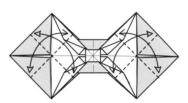

20 Start to fold a crane on each side. First, fold preliminary bases.

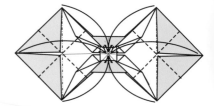

21 Fold and unfold the edges to the center on top layer only, to make creases for the next step.

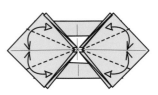

22 Petal fold.

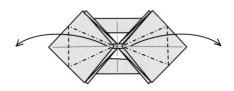

23 Mountain fold the flaps in the middle away from the center at the same time that the mid-section layers come together. This forms matching petal folds.

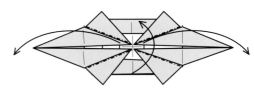

24 Now there are two bird bases connected in the middle. Open the middle flaps so that the bird bases align side by side, connected at the top.

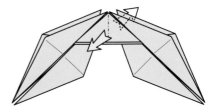

25 Inside reverse fold, and sink along the folded edges.

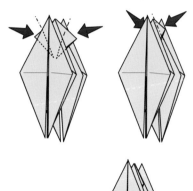

26 Narrow the flaps for the neck and tail of the crane (both sides, front and back). Repeat on the second crane.

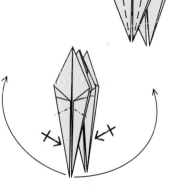

27 Inside reverse fold the neck and tail. Repeat on the second crane.

28 Inside reverse the head. Repeat on the second crane. Open the wings to make the model tridimensional.

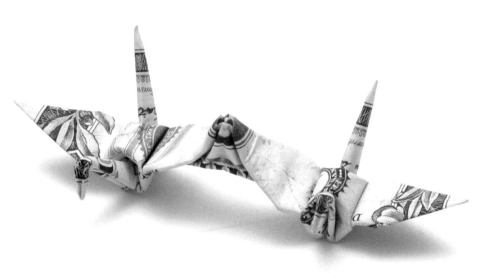

CRAB

Tip: wet the model with a damp paper towel, sponge, or a light mist spray and use a binder clip to clamp thick layers. This will help to retain the model's shape when dry, while folding a thick section

1   Using a ruler, divide the paper into equal fifths. Mark with a pinch or the dot of a pen.

2   Fold in half.

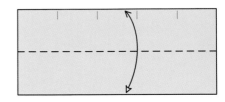

3   Crease into fifths (using the marks) and unfold.

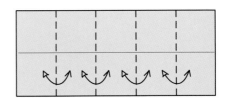

4   Crease each fifth in half and unfold.

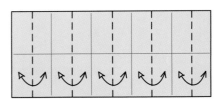

5 Valley fold on the first fifth.

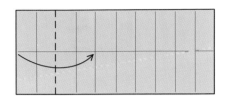

6 Crease from corner to corner and unfold.

7 Crease from corner to corner and unfold.

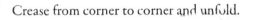

8 Collapse using the existing creases into something like a water bomb base.

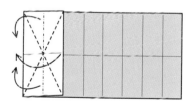

9 Inside reverse fold so that the edges are flush.

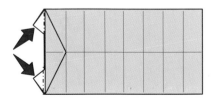

10 Inside reverse fold once again so that the edges are flush.

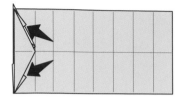

11 Repeat steps 6 to 10 on the remaining fifths.

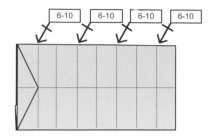

12 Fold two flaps to one side, and three to the other. Rotate the model.

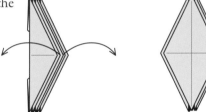

13 Find the pivot point: feel the point where the thickness changes. At that point, inside reverse all the layers on each side at once.

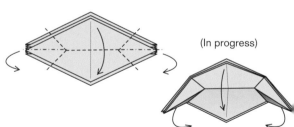

(In progress)

14 Open slightly and view from the side.

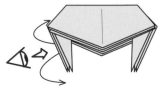

15 Fold the flaps to the opposite side.

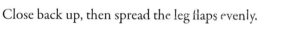

16 Rabbit ear fold. Arrange the flaps as needed.

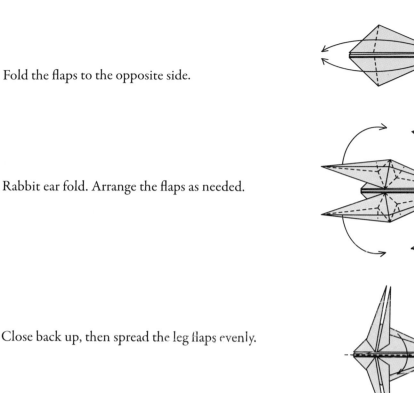

17 Close back up, then spread the leg flaps evenly.

18 Repeat steps 14 to 17 on the other side. Shape the pincers: outside reverse the top layer of the inner flaps.

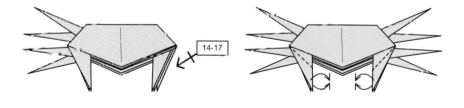

14-17

19 Fold flaps down along the folded edge.

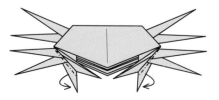

20 Fold up the top layer of the head. Tuck the two bottom layers under, then round the middle layers over the bottom layers to the crab's underside.

Top layer
Middle two layers
Bottom two layers

21 Crease to shape the carapace: mountain fold through the center, then valley fold the sides.

22 Push the back to make an inside reverse fold.

23 Lift the front edges to create eyes. Shape the pincers and legs as shown.

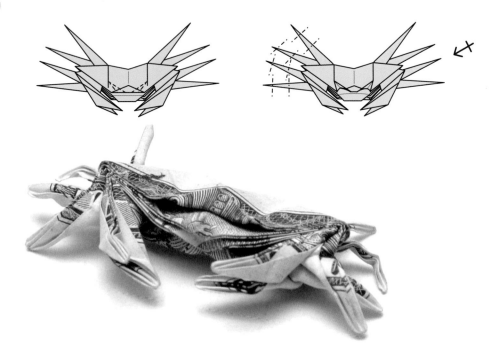

CAMERA

Tip: the key to folding this model is very sharp, precise creases. Use tweezers to manipulate the paper in tight spaces.

1. Fold the paper horizontally into equal eighths in a series of valley folds. First, fold in half and unfold.

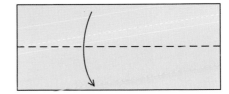

2. Fold and unfold.

3. Fold and unfold.

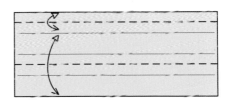

4. Fold and unfold.

5 Fold and unfold.

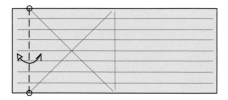

6 Mountain fold edges along center crease line. Unfold.

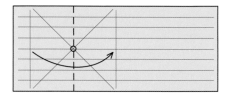

7 Fold between the points where the creases intersect the edges and unfold.

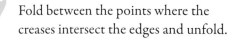

8 Valley fold as shown.

9 Inside reverse fold.

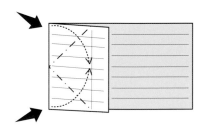

10 Fold between the points where the ²/₈ and ⁶/₈ horizontal lines intersect with the edge. Unfold.

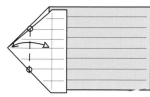

11 Fold between the points where the ³/₈ and ⁵/₈ horizontal lines intersects with the edge. Make sharp creases, folding both ways (valley and mountain). Unfold.

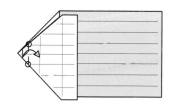

12 Spread sink using existing creases.

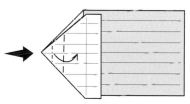

13 Valley fold vertically, between the points where the folded edges intersect the raw edges.

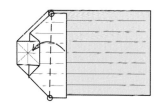

14 Pinch the center of the raw edge on the top and bottom.

15 Valley fold along the vertical 1/4 of the way from the folded edge.

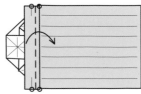

16 Valley fold along the vertical along 1/4 of the way from the raw edge.

17 Open the entire flap to the left.

18 Squash to flatten the model.

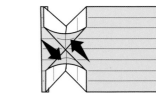

19 Turn the model over.

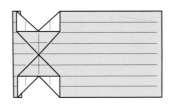

20 Valley fold the edges along the top and bottom 1/8 horizontal crease line.

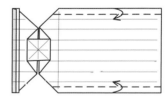

21 Fold and unfold mountain crease on the diagonal and at the same time pinch the center crease. Start from the top right corner of small triangle.

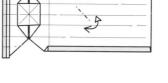

22 Fold and unfold mountain crease on the diagonal and at the same time pinch the center crease.

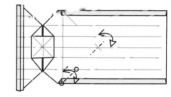

23 Valley fold using existing horizontal creases.

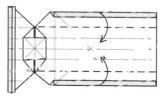

24 Inside reverse fold.

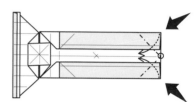

25 Valley fold and unfold all layers.

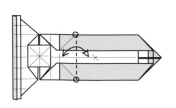

26 Valley fold all layers. Unfold.

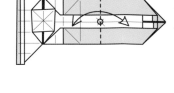

27 Fold and unfold top layer only. Note: it is easier if you open the flap part way.

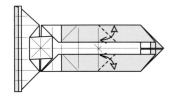

28 Valley fold all layers between the points where the diagonal crease intersects with the edge. Unfold.

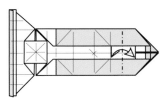

29 Mountain fold and unfold all layers creating a vertical crease exactly in the middle between the crease made in the previous step and the folded edge.

30 Rotate 90°. Magnified view for next steps.

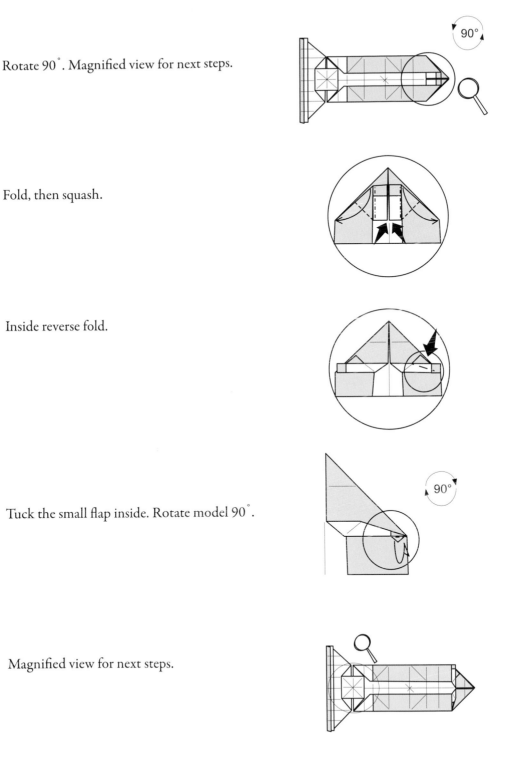

31 Fold, then squash.

32 Inside reverse fold.

33 Tuck the small flap inside. Rotate model 90°.

34 Magnified view for next steps.

35 Fold, then squash.

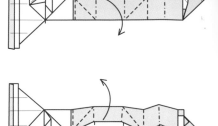

36 Start to fold the camera box.

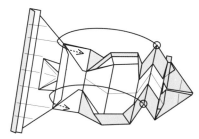

37 In progress.

38 Insert the points inside the pocket, creating a lid for the box. This is the body of the camera.

39 See next steps for the details of the buttons and flash.

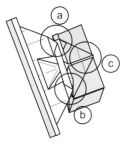

40 Shape the buttons …

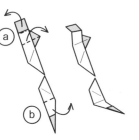 

…and the flash.

41 Swivel down the top layer. This will be the camera lens, and the swivel will help you shape it.

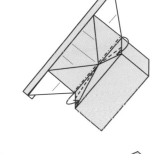

42 Form the lens by curling the paper (around a pencil) and wrapping the ends together. Insert the tab into the pocket to secure.

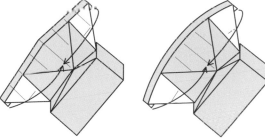

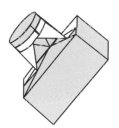

BUTTERFLY

1 Fold in half, horizontally and vertically. Unfold after each fold. This will create a long horizontal and a short vertical creases.

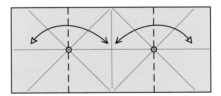

2 Fold the edges along the short vertical crease and unfold.

3 Create vertical creases through the intersection points of the diagonal creases.

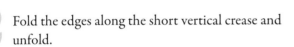

4 Fold in the middle of the creases. Unfold.

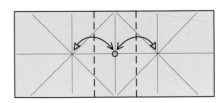

5 Create a short diagonal crease. Turn over.

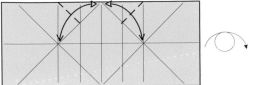

6 Fold in the middle of the creases. Unfold.

7 Create a short crease between the intersection points. Turn over.

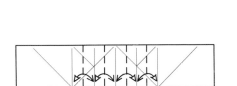

8 Collapse the center using the existing creases. See next step as a reference for the result.

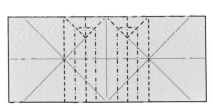

9 Fold down the tip. Fold it again.

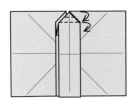

10 Turn over.

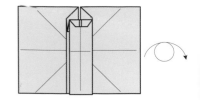

11 Valley fold the flaps from the intersection of the crease to the edge as far as they can go.

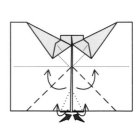

12 Open and spread the layer, then squash fold.

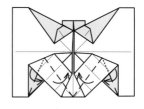

13 Swivel fold.

14 Pleat fold up to the points.

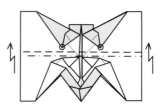

15 The next steps will focus on splitting the wings.

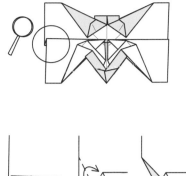

16 Fold the top layer, then flatten by creating an additional crease on the bottom layer.

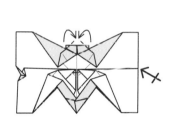

17 Repeat the previous step on the other side. Fold the corners of the head inside.

18 Fold to create the body and make the model tridimensional. Finish the tail: wrap it to one side and tuck it into the pocket. Turn over.

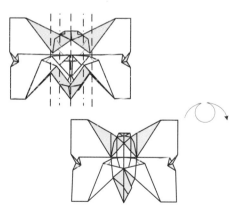

FROG

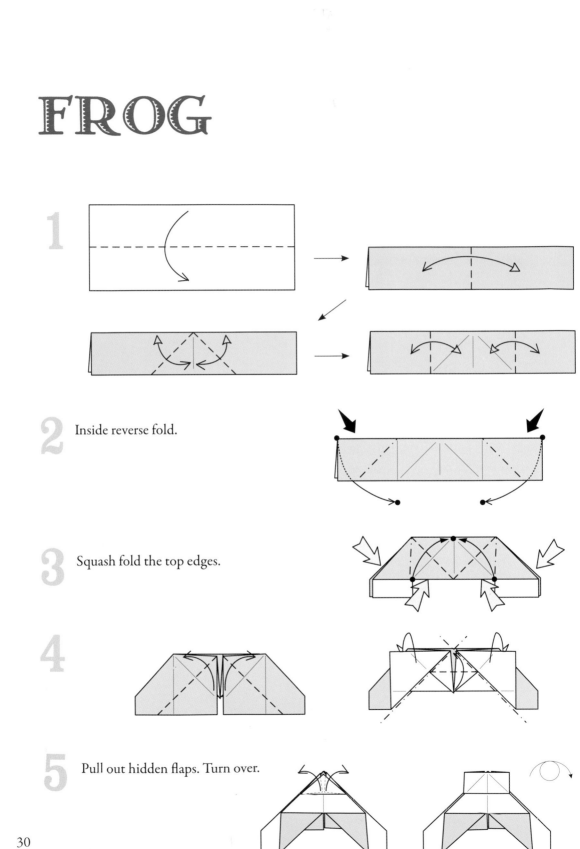

2 Inside reverse fold.

3 Squash fold the top edges.

4

5 Pull out hidden flaps. Turn over.

6 Outside reverse fold (open the model part way for this). On the rear, the fold originates underneath another layer.

(Rear view)

7 Open to view inside. Petal fold.

(Petal fold)

8 Collapse the top section to make legs. Closed sink the first mountain fold, closest to the body. Inside reverse fold the two subsequent flaps.

9 Tuck the top layer inside: starting from the folded edge inside, fold about half of the flap inside.

10 Tuck the flaps inside, one layer at a time.

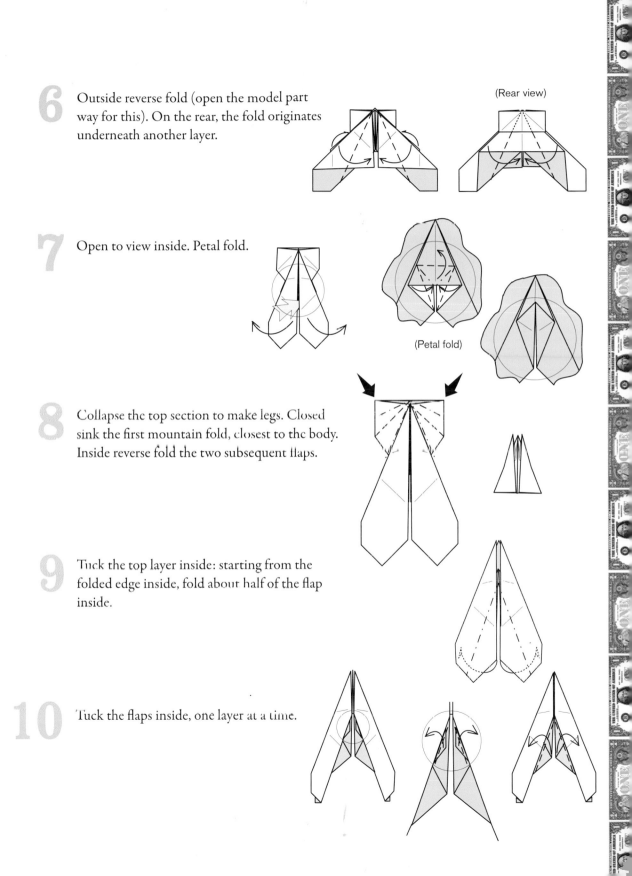

11 Open the top section and shift the sides (see picture) and flatten. Turn the model over.

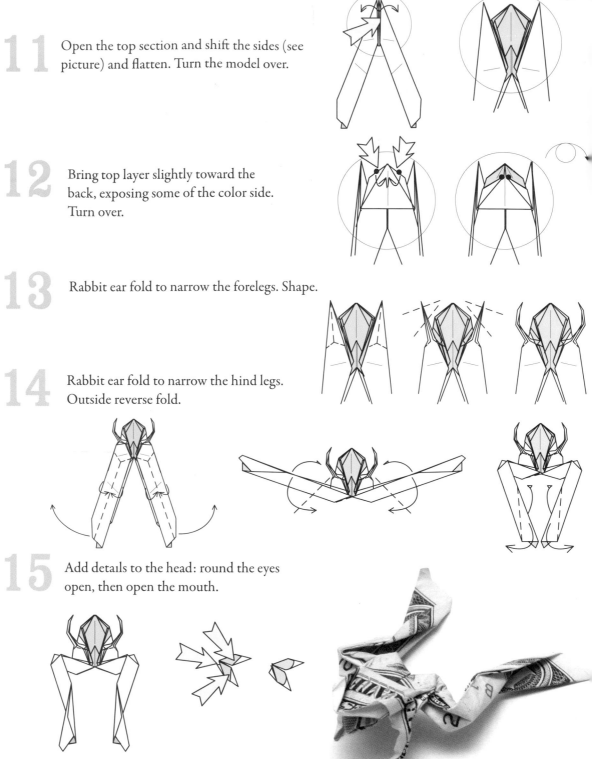

12 Bring top layer slightly toward the back, exposing some of the color side. Turn over.

13 Rabbit ear fold to narrow the forelegs. Shape.

14 Rabbit ear fold to narrow the hind legs. Outside reverse fold.

15 Add details to the head: round the eyes open, then open the mouth.

(View from bottom)

PENGUIN

Use the practice money included with this kit until you feel confident enough to use real dollar bills. When you use real $1 bills, the printed pattern on the reverse will form the model's eyes.

1. If using real money, start with the George Washington side up. Fold in half. Unfold.

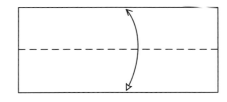

2. Fold the edges along the crease.

3. Fold the edges along the crease. Unfold.

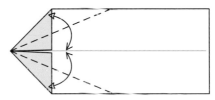

4. Fold the edges along the further crease lines to create angle bisectors. No need to fold all the way, since these are just references for the next step. Unfold.

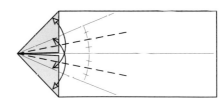

5 Fold the edges along the creases created in the previous step.

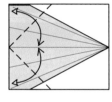

6 Fold in half, bringing the tip to the far edge.

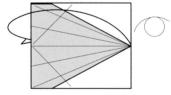

7 Fold the edges along the center crease line. Crease well. Unfold.

8 Fold the tip toward the back, reversing the crease from mountain to a valley. Turn over.

9 Inside reverse fold on existing creases.

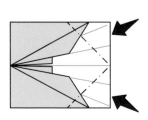

10 Fold the large flap on the back under, towards the tip.

11 Fold in half.

12 Fold the top layer, pivoting from the middle of the edge and the first crease, and aligning the edge to the corner. Fold the other side to match.

13 Fold the top layer from the same pivot point of previous step to the same corner. Fold the other side to match.

14 Lift slightly to see the reference point under the layer. Valley fold, starting from the same pivot point to the reference point shown. Crease well. Unfold. Fold the other side to match.

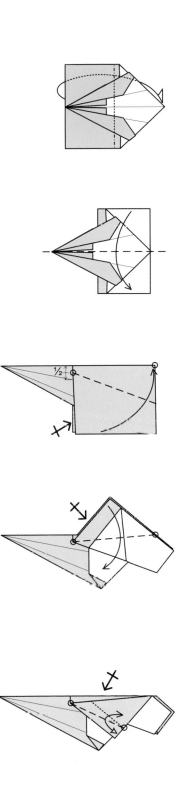

15 Unfold to the position in step 13.

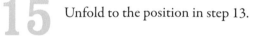

16 Swivel the paper in between the layers. Create a new crease to flatten. Fold the other side to match.

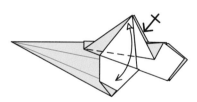

17 Valley fold along the edge. Unfold. Repeat on the other side.

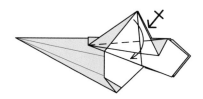

18 Valley fold along the folded edge. Repeat on the other side.

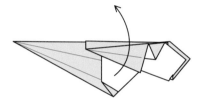

19 Open.

20 Fold the tip as far as it can go, creasing well from corner to corner. Unfold.

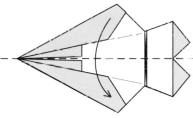

21 Open sink. Use the creases made on the previous step. Open the model partially so that you can execute this step.

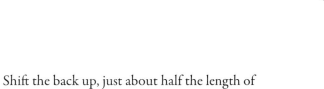

22 Fold in half.

23 Shift the back up, just about half the length of the short edge. See next step.

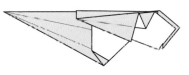

24 Raise the back, just about half the length of the short edge. See next step for detailed view.

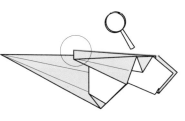

37

25 Inside reverse the tiny corner. A second inside reverse allows an even distribution of layers so this corner stays put.

26 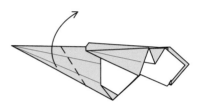 Valley fold the head so that the edge is almost perpendicular to the body and against the small corner created in the previous step.

27 Crease well. Unfold.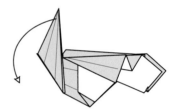

28 Crimp fold. First, reverse the crease on the other side to become valley. Start the crimp.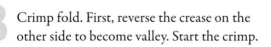

29 Find a good position for the head and complete the crimp. Rotate 90°.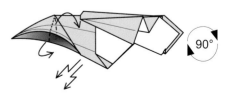

30 Open sink the head.

31 Narrow the belly: fold at about half the distance between the creases. Tuck both sides inside.

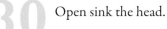

32 Open the wing.

33 Valley fold so that the upper edge is nearly horizontal. Do not fold past the belly. Repeat on the other side.

34 Swivel fold. Start from the top reference point: as you try to flatten, new creases will be made. Repeat on the other side.

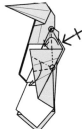

39

35 Asymmetrical inside reverse fold. At the tail end, the fold should come to a point. Repeat on the other side.

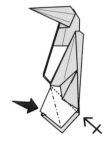

36 Lift the flap up to view inside for the next step.

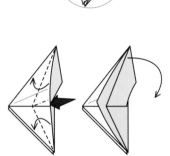

37 Inside reverse fold. Close.

38 Repeat on the other side.

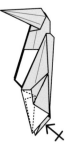

39 Lift the feet out and then open the sides of the belly to work on the tail.

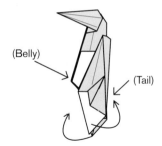

(Belly)

(Tail)

40 Crimp fold the tail: mountain fold toward the back, and valley fold just enough to allow the tail to jut out slightly. Close.

(Belly)

(Tail)

(Detailed view of the tail from the inside)

41 Lift the foot to shape it from the inside.

(Tail)

42 Inside reverse fold.

(Inside reverse fold created in step 37)

(Tail)

43 Valley fold, allowing the paper behind to swivel. Fold the feet in half to flatten. Repeat on the other foot.

44 Tuck flaps inside to narrow the belly. Crimp the beak.

EAGLE

1 Fold in half, short edge to short edge. Fold bottom edge to the folded edge. Repeat on the other side.

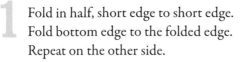  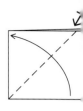

2 Open the back layer. Fold the edges to the folded edge. Unfold. Turn over.

3 Valley fold the flaps on the back along the edge. Unfold. Turn over.

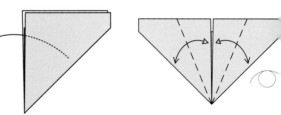

4 Fold the creases created on the previous step to the folded edge. Refolding the previous crease into a mountain may make this easier. Unfold.

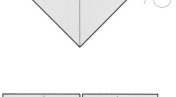 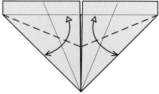

5 Crease from the intersection of the creases to the corners.

6 Rabbit ear fold, using existing creases plus one additional mountain crease, to flatten.

7 Fold each flap as far as it goes. The corner will align on the crease line. Unfold.

8 Rabbit ear fold. Create new valley folds from the intersection of the creases and the corner to do this.

9 Fold the flaps as far as they can go.

10 Starting from the tip of each flap, fold the edges to the folded edges, extending the crease up to the reference points. These will become the wings. From this step on, the model will not lie flat.

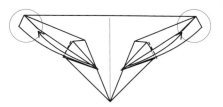

11 Move the flaps to the other direction.

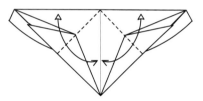

12 Gently valley fold, aligning the edges with the crease line. Refolding the mountain crease in the center may make this easier. Crease well. Unfold. Do not touch the flaps that are not flat.

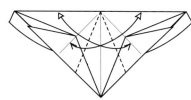

13 Valley fold the edges to the new creases on the opposite side. Unfold.

14 Fold in half.

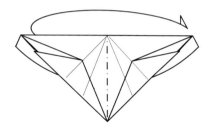

15 Valley fold on the creases created in step 13. Pay attention to the references for the next steps. Repeat on the other side.

(References for next step)

16 Valley fold through the center and bringing the point where the crease ends to the folded edge. Repeat on the other side.

(References between the layers)

17 Fold the flap down. Repeat on the other side. Make sure reference points line up with edges shown.

(References from step 15)

18 Swivel fold. Only one crease exists (the one on the back). The others will need to be created, along the edge and the last one to flatten. Repeat on the other side.

19 Swivel fold. No crease exists for this step. Start by aligning the edge to the folded edge (on what will be the head). Then, swivel the paper on the wing. Repeat on the other side.

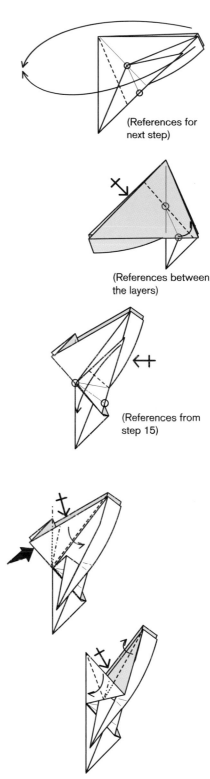

20 Lift swivel fold to find the pocket inside, and tuck the flap in. Repeat on the other side.

21 Fold the flap back up. Repeat on the other side. Open the model from behind.

22 Fold and unfold to crease between the reference points. It may be easier to fold from the back.

23 Create these creases by lifting the edges up. Don't flatten yet.

24 Fold the corners in, then collapse the tail.

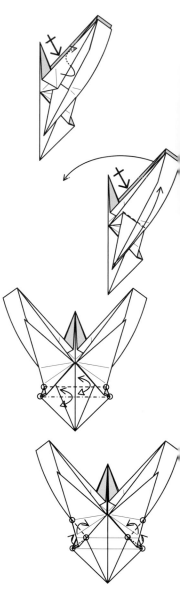

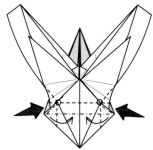

25 Turn over.

26 Create new valley creases along the edges under the top layer. Fold in half, allowing the tail to lift on the new creases.

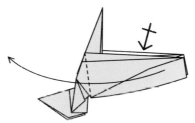

27 Rabbit ear to fold the entire wing (it is very thick close to the tail). Repeat on the other side.

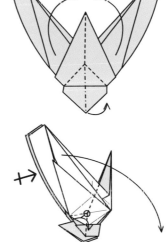

28 Valley fold just the top layer back (leave the leg in place). Repeat on the other side.

29 Open the tail slightly. View from the underside.

47

30 Valley fold so that the thick edges are parallel to the center line. Press all layers closer to the back to keep tail in this position.

31 Begin final shaping of head, talons, and wings.

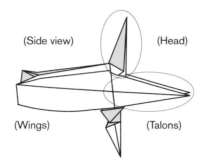

(Side view)   (Head)   (Top view)

(Wings)   (Talons)

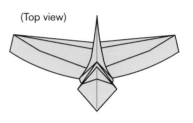

32 Outside reverse fold, then crimp and inside reverse the tip of the beak.

33 Fashion talons with sequence of mountain folds. For finished eagle, round and open the sides of the wings.

SHARK

1 Fold in half. Unfold.

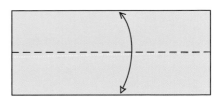

2 Fold the short edge along the long ones. Unfold.

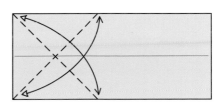

3 Flip the paper over, top to bottom.

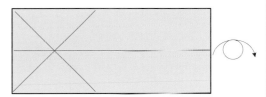

4 Fold the short edge along the long ones. Unfold.

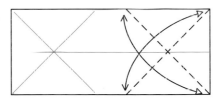

5 Mountain fold on the intersection. Unfold.

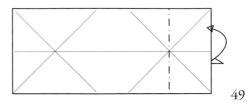

6 Fold the edges to the creases created in step 2, and crease only up to the center line. Unfold.

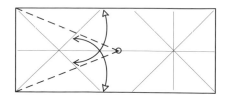

7 Collapse the waterbomb base.

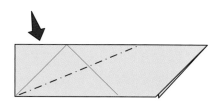

8 Fold in half.

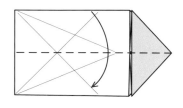

9 Inside reverse fold using existing creases.

10 Inside reverse fold using existing creases.

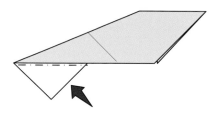

11 Inside reverse fold creating new creases, so that the edges align.

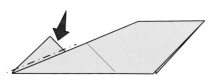

12 Inside reverse fold to make the smaller dorsal fin. Use your judgment for the size.

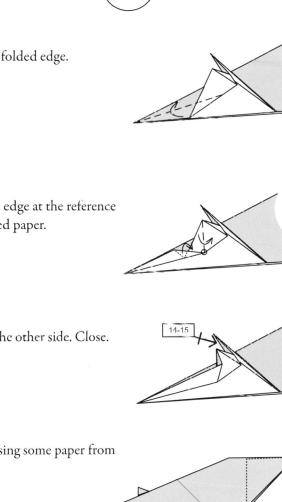

13 Open slightly to work on the inside of the tail fin.

14 Fold the cut edge along the folded edge.

15 Swivel fold: hold the folded edge at the reference point, releasing some trapped paper.

16 Repeat steps 14 and 15 on the other side. Close.

14-15

17 Pull out the two flaps, releasing some paper from inside.

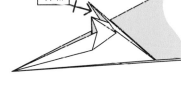

18 Pivoting from the top corner, bring the top edge to where crease meets the edge. Crease well. Unfold.

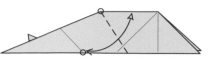

19 Move the two flaps inside, back to the position in step 17.

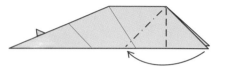

20 Open the head part way. Put back creases created in step 18, reversing the one on the back to become mountain.

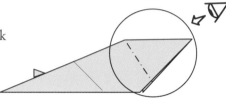

21 Start a new crease on the inside, to create a crimp fold. Close, and flatten.

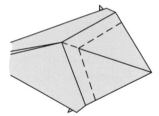

22 Crease well. Open again and look inside.

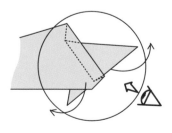

23 Fold the corners to the center and crease well. Unfold.

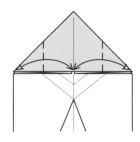

24 Valley fold the top layer only. It will not lie flat.

25 Bring the sides together using the creases inside and pull the tip up. New creases are necessary to flatten.

26 Valley fold the corners, using existing creases.

27 Pop up the point in the center of the model. Using the existing creases, fold in half, pushing the head inside.

(Pop-up from the back)

28 Valley fold between the references. Crease well.

29 Open sink.

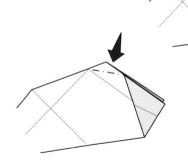

30 Pull the sink open slightly.

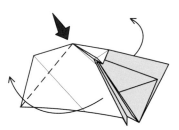

31 Push the tip forward.

32 Push to return to the original position (before step 27).

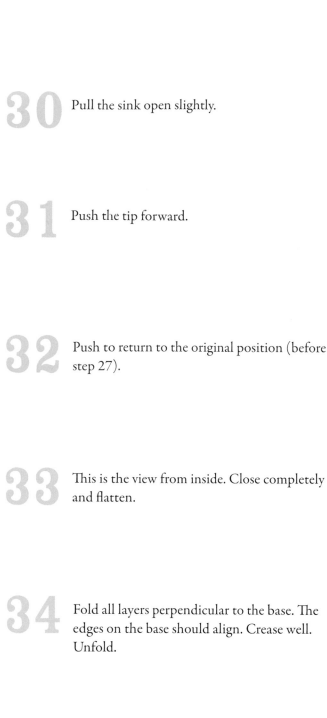

33 This is the view from inside. Close completely and flatten.

34 Fold all layers perpendicular to the base. The edges on the base should align. Crease well. Unfold.

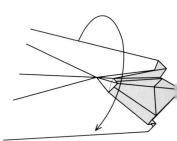

35 Fold on the crease made in the previous step and pleat.

36 Fold an angle bisector, edge to edge. Crease well. Unfold. Unfold the pleat made on the previous step.

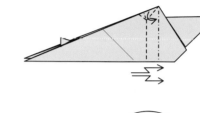

37 Crimp fold. Move the top towards one of the sides, to allow room for the crimp to go inside the model.

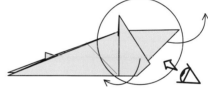

38 Open the head to look inside.

39 Valley fold the flap together with the layer under, but not the lowest layer. See next step.

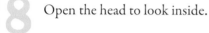

40 Swivel and flatten. Repeat on the other side. Fold the model back up.

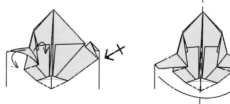

41 Inside reverse fold to define the pectoral fin. Repeat on the other side too.

55

42 Inside reverse again, on the inside. Repeat on the other side.

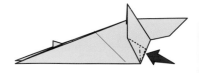

43 Fold the top layer inside. Repeat on the other side.

44 Work on the tail fins: first, turn the model over.

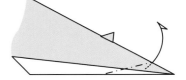

45 Mountain fold the top fin to the inside.

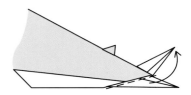

46 Fold the bottom fin around the first fin.

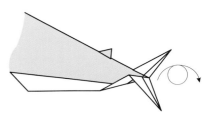

47 Valley fold fin, creating a lock. See next step for result. Turn over.

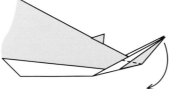

48 Tuck the excess paper between the layers.

49 Open the head to look inside.

50 Keeping the top partially open, pull out one layer to make the mouth. Create a crease so that the lower jaw opens. Create another crease, to keep the jaw open.

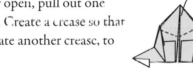

51 The head and the body are now tridimensional. Pull the pectoral fins outward slightly to round the belly for the final shaping.

SCORPION

1   Fold in half. Unfold.

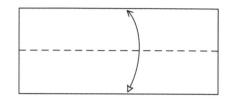

2   Fold the short edge to the long ones. Unfold. Turn over, flipping top to bottom. Valley fold on the intersection. Unfold.

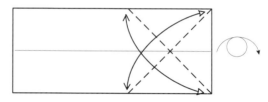

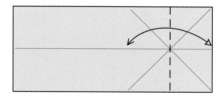

3   Crease the angle bisectors by aligning the edges to the creases. Turn over, flipping top to bottom.

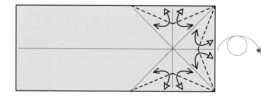

4   Crease the angle bisectors by aligning the creases to the creases.

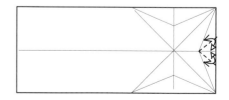

5 Collapse the waterbomb base.

6 Inside reverse fold the inner flaps using existing creases.

7 Pivoting from the intersection of the creases, fold point A and align the crease lines. Note that it will not reach the tip. No crease is created on this step, and the model will not lie flat.

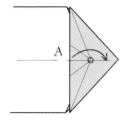

8 Bring the flaps to meet, then press the areas indicated to flatten, making new creases. The inner layer should lie flat on existing creases.

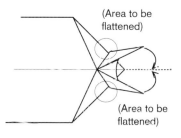

(Area to be flattened)

(Area to be flattened)

9 Valley fold using the crease on the layer inside as a reference, so that the flap will stretch out and flatten completely.

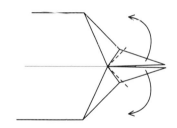

10   Detailed view.

11   Make these creases for a rabbit ear fold in the next step. After each crease, make the mirror image on the opposite flap.

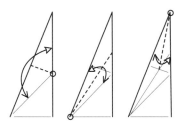

12   Rabbit ear fold. Crease well. Unfold. Repeat on the other flap.

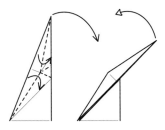

13   Valley fold the top layer to open up flap; press the center to flatten. Petal fold, then fold in half. Repeat sequence on other flap.

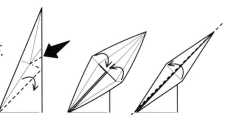

14   Create a small crimp fold inside so that the flap aligns with the edge. Repeat on the other flap.

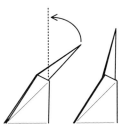

15 Turn over.

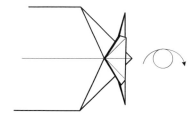

16 Fold the edges of the top layer to align with the center crease, from the tip to the folded edges hidden underneath. The model will not lie flat.

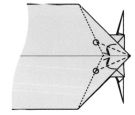

17 Release the layer that is trapped.

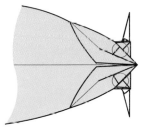

18 Swivel fold.

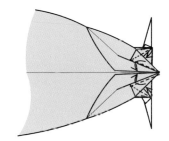

19 Shift the edges around the folded edges, allowing some paper to stretch to flatten.

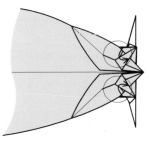

20 Turn over.

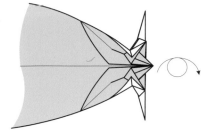

21 Start creasing along the edges from the sides. Crease to connect the references. Let the head fold over.

22 Flatten the area indicated. The model should lie flat.

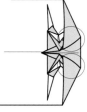

23 Fold the entire flap to the back.

24 Mountain crease the folded edge.

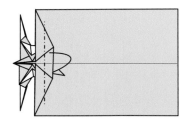

25 Pleat. Start the first crease slightly bellow the edge, not on it.

26 Detailed view of the pleats.

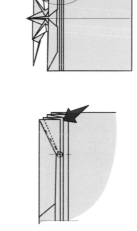

27 Inside reverse folding asymmetrically, starting from a point parallel to the center line, and ending in a point.

28 Continue reverse folding so that the edges becomes flush.

29 Repeat the inside reverse folds on the other pleats.

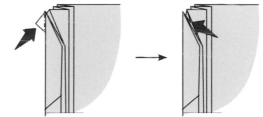

30 Repeat steps 27 to 29 on the other side.

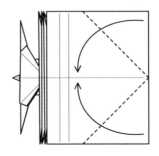

27-29

31 Pleat fold. The first mountain should align with the folded edge. The valley fold should leave the same gap used on step 26. Unfold. Turn over.

32 Fold the edges to the center line.

33 Fold the edges to the center crease, only to the first perpendicular crease. Unfold.

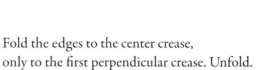

34 Pleat on existing creases.

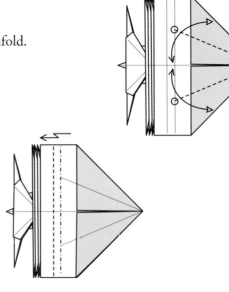

35 Fold the edges to the center crease, allowing some of the paper to lift. The model will not lie flat.

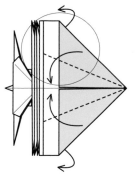

36 Press the area indicated, creating new creases to flatten.

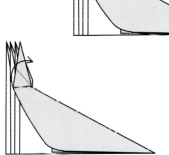

37 Fold upright to view the inside.

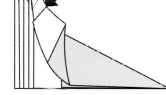

38 Push from back to pop up one layer, eliminating the edge on the front and defining the edges on this side.

39 Press the area indicated, creating new creases to flatten. The model should lie flat now.

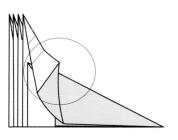

40 Fold from corner to corner.

41 Repeat steps 36 to 40 on the other side.

36-40

42 Fold the edge almost to the center crease of the tail.

43 Fold the legs back out along the center line. Repeat this sequence on the other side.

44 Turn over.

45 Rabbit ear the tail to lift it up.

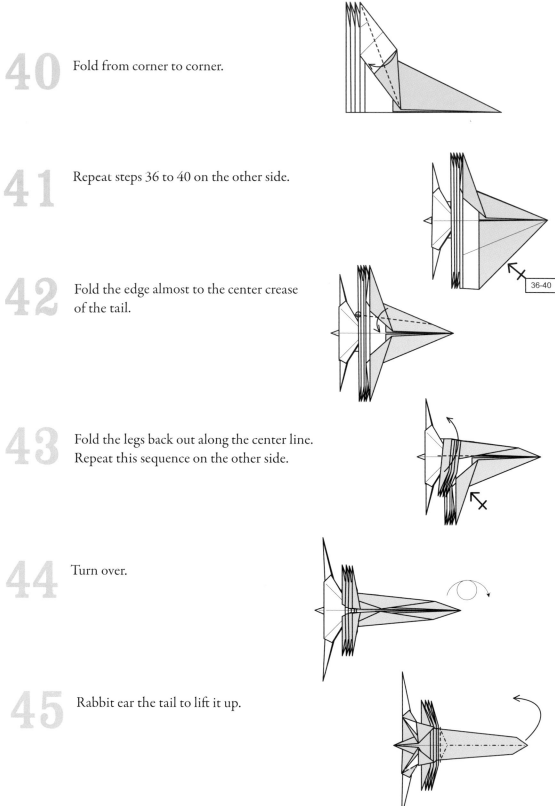

46 The next steps show the shaping of the tail, legs, pincers, and head.

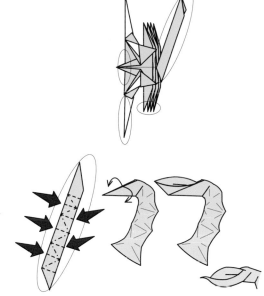

47 Start by pinching the tail into a series of water bomb bases to make segments; curve; open the tip for the venom bulb; pinch and curve to make the stinger.

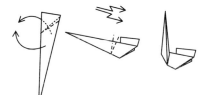

48 Make leg articulations with valley and mountain creases.

49 For the pincers, make an outside reverse fold, then crimp and leave the flap slightly open.

50 Fold the head down as far as possible. Fold the mouthparts (the tip) forward.

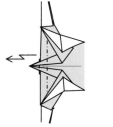

KOI FISH

Use the practice money included with this kit until you feel confident enough to use real dollar bills. When you use real $1 bills, the printed pattern on the reverse will form the model's eyes.

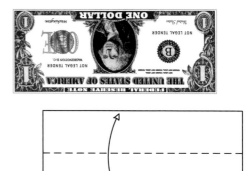

1 If using real money, start with the face side visible, but position the bill so George Washington is upside down. Fold in half lengthwise and unfold.

2 Fold the short edge to the long edges and crease only up to the central horizontal crease. Unfold.

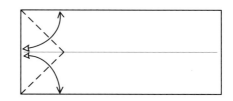

3 Fold short edges to the central horizontal crease only up to the diagonals made in step 2. Unfold.

4 Fold vertically at the intersection of the creases. Unfold.

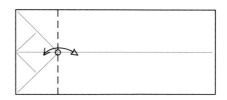

5 Pinch midway between the reference points.

6 Pinch midway between the reference points.

7 Valley fold midway between the reference points. Unfold.

8 Pleat using the creases, reversing the last crease from valley to mountain fold.

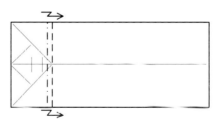

9 Mountain fold vertically along the folded edge. Unfold. Unfold the pleat back to the position in previous step.

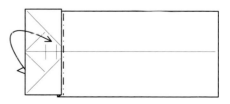

10 Fold the edges to the central horizontal crease, creasing between the vertical edge and the pleat crease line.

11 Pre-crease for a future step. Mountain fold the raw edge along the diagonal, from the corner to the horizontal line.

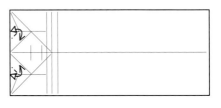

12 Pre-crease for a future step. Mountain fold parallel to the diagonal created in step 3.

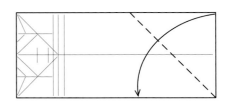

13 Fold short edge along the long edge.

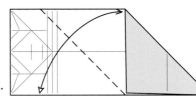

14 Fold the corner to the long edge and unfold. Unfold the flap made in step 13.

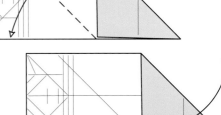

15 Repeat steps 13 and 14 on the other side, creating mirror-image creases.

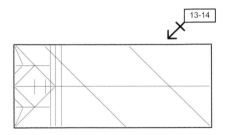

16 Fold and unfold.

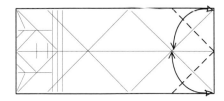

17 Fold in half (crease to crease).

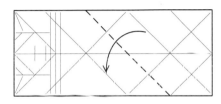

18 Fold edge to edge, unfold. Unfold the flap created in the previous step.

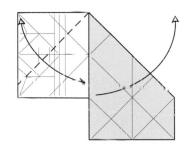

19 Repeat steps 17 and 18 on the other side, creating mirror-image creases.

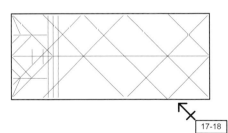

20 Narrow the grid by folding in half (crease to crease) and unfolding.

21 Narrow the grid by folding in half (crease to crease) and unfolding once more. Turn over.

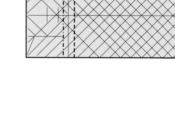

22 On the color (green) side, pleat using the existing creases (created in steps 7 to 9).

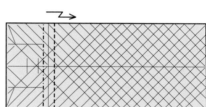

23 Find the small triangle immediately next to the folded edge, along the center. Using that triangle as a reference, mountain fold the crease that goes along its side. Unfold the pleat created in the previous step.

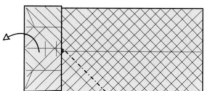

24 Extend the mountain crease started in the previous step. Mountain fold the next crease too.

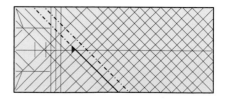

25 Bring the edges together creating a valley crease in the middle. Be as precise as possible and crease well.

26 Unfold the long flap on the back.

27 Valley fold using the next crease line. Turn over.

28 Bring folded edge to the crease line, allowing the flap to flip out from behind.

29 Turn over. Repeat the pleating process (steps 24 to 28) to the end of the dollar bill.

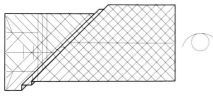

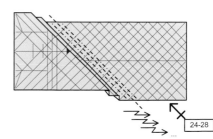

24-28

30 Unfold everything. Flatten the dollar bill as much as possible to crease the other side to avoid paper creep.

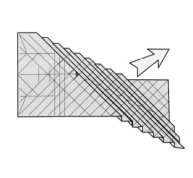

31 Narrow the gridlines going in the other direction using the same technique described in steps 24 to 30.

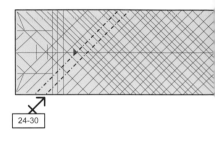

32 Pleat again, but this time alternating sides. Pleat one side, then the other (all layers) and so on. The result should be symmetrical.

33 Locate the crease created in step 9. Valley fold the entire side, which will become the head of the koi fish. Crease well.

34 Turn over. Rotate 90° clockwise.

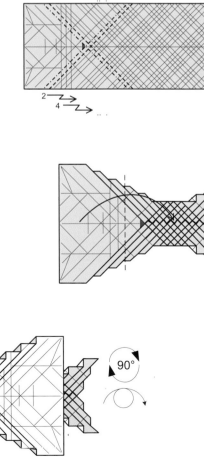

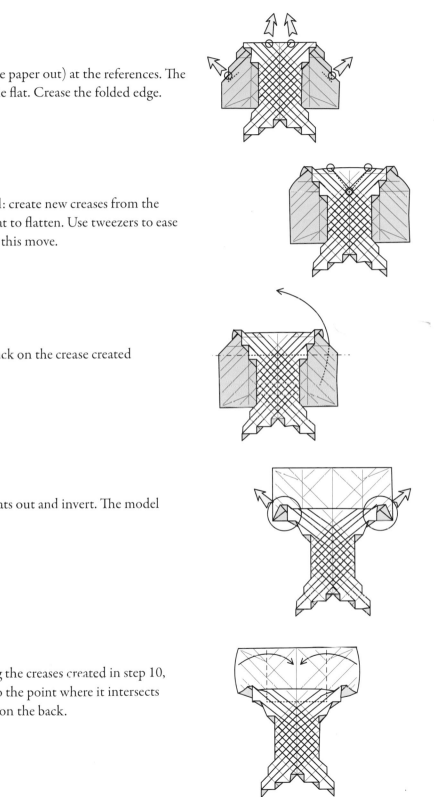

35 Unpleat (pull the paper out) at the references. The model will not lie flat. Crease the folded edge.

36 Adust the model: create new creases from the inside of the pleat to flatten. Use tweezers to ease the paper up for this move.

37 Fold the head back on the crease created in step 7.

38 Pull the two pleats out and invert. The model will not lie flat.

39 Valley fold using the creases created in step 10, from the edge to the point where it intersects the folded edge on the back.

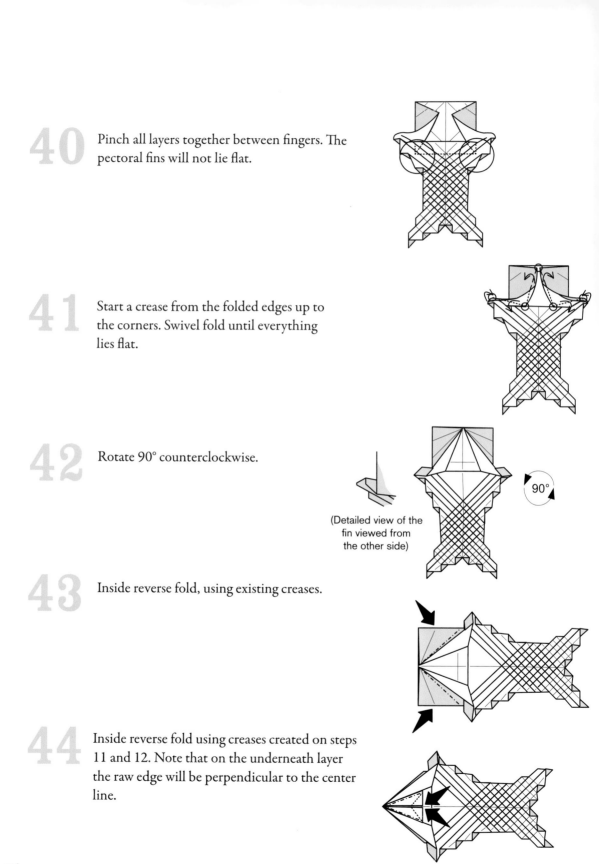

40   Pinch all layers together between fingers. The pectoral fins will not lie flat.

41   Start a crease from the folded edges up to the corners. Swivel fold until everything lies flat.

42   Rotate 90° counterclockwise.

(Detailed view of the fin viewed from the other side)

90°

43   Inside reverse fold, using existing creases.

44   Inside reverse fold using creases created on steps 11 and 12. Note that on the underneath layer the raw edge will be perpendicular to the center line.

45 Fold in half gently.

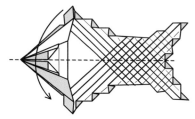

46 Crimp the head. Mountain fold on the folded edge on the back of the head. Valley fold between the reference points. Grasp the layers with tweezers along the guides shown and twist to mark the folds.

47 Lift the top layer to find the reference point. Notice that underneath, the head connects to the fin. Valley crease only up to that point. Don't crease further than that.

(Detailed view)

48 Start the crimp where the previous crease ended. Grasp the layer up to the reference point and twist to the right, using the edge of the tweezer to mark the crease. The printed pattern of the dollar bill should show, forming the eyes of the koi.

49 To lock, mountain fold between the landmarks indicated (from the end of the crease on the top of the head to the corner of the fin). Repeat steps 47 and 48 on the other side. At this point the head should be tridimensional and will not lie flat.

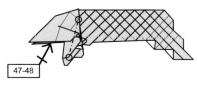

47-48

50 Look at the head from the top. Use the printed pattern as a reference; fold on line between the green and white. Make sure the fold is centered and crease well (use tweezers to pinch layers flat in 3-D areas).

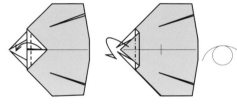

51 Use your judgment for this fold. Fold the tip forward, leaving a small edge, then fold the tip under. Crease well. Turn over to work on the whiskers from underneath.

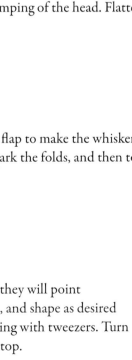

52 First, open the layers that might have gotten trapped during the crimping of the head. Flatten to make it smooth.

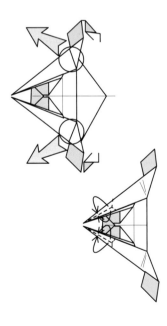

53 Rabbit ear to thin the flap to make the whiskers. Use the tweezers to mark the folds, and then to pinch into shape.

54 Move the whiskers so they will point forward along the lips, and shape as desired by pinching and bending with tweezers. Turn over to the view from top.

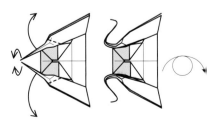

55 Shape the lips with tweezers: first, mountain crease the center down. Then valley fold the corners back to lock.

56 Fold the pectoral fins out. Inserting a pen under the body, press the koi against it and round. Round the head, too, using tweezers to bend. Option: use tweezers to make little pinches to create a spiny back, which adds to the koi's beauty and realism.

57 To shape the tail, open the layers and look at the inside. Rotate for proper orientation.

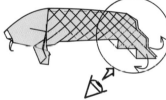

58 Pull out the first pleat, easing the paper from the center. Flatten, creating a new crease on the inside which will become the new folded edge.

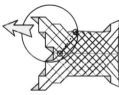

59 Fan out three pleats. Open and create a new crease inside to flatten.

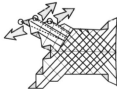

60 Fold back between the reference points, pushing out slightly to create a rounded edge. Crease well. Turn over. Gently fold in half.

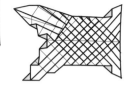

61 Fold up, from below the tip of the tail to the end of the second pleat.

62 Press tail back slightly, while rounding the back. Tuck the excess at the bottom inside, rounding the body. Make sure the tail stays up.

63 Curve the tip of the tail. Curl. Repeat steps 59 to 61 on the other fin, but position this fin down. Tuck the excess inside and curl as with the top fin. Finish shaping and rounding.

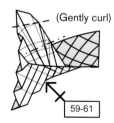

(Gently curl)

59-61